Let's Get Active™

LET'S PLAY

BASKETBALL

Shane McFee

PowerKiDS
press™

New York

Published in 2008 by The Rosen Publishing Group, Inc.
29 East 21st Street, New York, NY 10010

First Edition

Editors: Jennifer Way and Nicole Pristash
Book Design: Greg Tucker
Photo Researcher: Nicole Pristash

Photo Credits: Cover © Dennis MacDonald; p. 5 © www.iStockphoto.com/Stacy Barnett; pp. 7, 13, 21 © Getty Images; pp. 9, 17 Shutterstock.com; p. 11 © www.iStockphoto.com/Rob Friedman; p. 15 © Jeff Kaufman/Getty Images; p. 19 © Thomas Northcut/Getty Images.

Library of Congress Cataloging-in-Publication Data

McFee, Shane.
   Let's play basketball / Shane McFee. — 1st ed.
      p. cm. — (Let's get active)
   Includes index.
   ISBN 978-1-4042-4193-0 (library binding)
   1. Basketball—Juvenile literature. I. Title.
   GV885.1.M4 2008
   796.323—dc22
                                                    2007034649

Manufactured in the United States of America

Contents

Basketball

Have you ever played basketball? Basketball is one of the most widely watched sports in the United States. It is a very common **spectator** sport. Many people watch **professional** basketball in the National Basketball Association. This is also called the NBA. Men's and women's **college** basketball is almost as widely watched as professional basketball.

Anyone can learn to play basketball. It is a great way to get exercise and to have fun with your friends!

You can play basketball on a team at school or in your town. You can also practice by yourself, like this girl. All you need is a hoop and a basketball.

5

Peach Baskets

A Canadian doctor and teacher named James Naismith invented basketball in 1891. Naismith noticed that his students were not in good shape during the winter. This was because they could not go outside to exercise in the snow. Naismith invented basketball as a form of indoor exercise.

Naismith nailed two wooden peach baskets to poles in his school's gym. The baskets hung 10 feet (3 m) in the air. Since the basketball had not been invented yet, Naismith's students played the game with a soccer ball!

Basketball has changed over the years. The game we play today is faster and harder than the game Naismith invented.

This is a photo of James Naismith (middle right) with his students, in 1891. These students made up the very first basketball team in history!

What You Need

All you really need to play basketball is a ball and a court. Courts are long, rectangular spaces with baskets at both ends. Indoor courts generally have wooden floors. Outdoor courts are generally made of blacktop. **Informal** games can be played on half courts. Half courts have only one basket for the players to shoot into. Soccer balls are no longer used to play basketball. Today's basketballs are orange. They **bounce** much better than soccer balls.

Safety is very important when playing basketball. Most players wear special shoes called high-tops. They keep your ankles safe because basketball players run and jump a lot.

Basketball hoops outside people's homes are used for informal games. This boy is practicing on his driveway.

Rules of the Game

Basketball games are **contests** between two teams. Each team has five players on the court at one time. The object of the game is to throw, or shoot, the ball into the other team's basket. Most shots are worth two points.

Players are not allowed to carry the ball. They have to move it down the court by bouncing it with their hands. This is called dribbling. They can also throw it to another player on their team. This is called passing.

Basketball games are timed. The team with the most points at the end of the game wins!

This player is shooting a free throw. A free throw is taken when a player on the other team breaks a rule. A free throw is worth one point.

The Referee

Most basketball games have at least one referee. The referee is an **official** who makes sure the game is played fairly. She can stop the game by blowing a **whistle**. This generally means a player has done something that is against the rules.

Players are not allowed to walk or run while holding the ball. This is called traveling. If a player travels, the referee will blow his whistle and give the ball to the other team. Players are also not allowed to hold, trip, or hit players on the other team. If this happens, the referee will call a **foul**.

Referees use their hands to call a foul. Each foul has its own signal, or sign.

The Players

Each player has a different position on the basketball court. The point guard is the team's **offensive** leader. He has to be excellent at passing and dribbling. The shooting guard is a fast player. He must be good at **defense**.

The power forward is a strong defensive player. She catches rebounds. Rebounds are missed shots that bounce off the basket. The small forward is generally the best shooter on the team. She must be ready to shoot from anywhere on the court. The center is the team's defensive leader. She blocks shots and catches rebounds.

In this game, the boy in the blue shirt is trying to stop the other player from shooting the ball. He is practicing good defense.

The Coach

Like most sports teams, every basketball team has a leader. The leader is called the coach. The coach works very closely with the players to help plan the team's **strategy**. A strategy is made up of plays. Plays are movements of players that make it hard for the other team to score. The point guard is the person who makes sure that the plays happen correctly and at the right moments.

Basketball coaches also lead the teams in practice. In practice, players do special exercises called drills. Drills help players get better at shooting, dribbling, and rebounding.

Coaches have a hard job. They must teach the players how to do their best. Coaches must also try to lead their team to success.

Teamwork and Sportsmanship

Basketball provides fun and exercise, but it also teaches you the value of teamwork. Teamwork is working together with others. Good basketball players cannot play alone. They need to pass the ball to their teammates.

Basketball also teaches you sportsmanship. Sportsmanship means being a good loser and a good winner. Good losers clap for the winners. Good winners do not brag to the losers. Sportsmanship also means not **cheating**. In basketball, cheating will lead to a foul. Fouls give the other team a chance to score points. In basketball, teamwork and sportsmanship go together.

Having good sportsmanship means being a good teammate. These girls are cheering for the other players on their team.

Meet LeBron James

LeBron James is one of the best players in the NBA. He is the small forward for the Cleveland Cavaliers. Even though he is a young player, James is the leader of his team. He made basketball history in Game 5 of the 2007 NBA Eastern Conference Finals. He scored 29 of his team's final 30 points!

James was already a famous basketball player before he even finished high school. Many people believe he will go down in basketball history as one of the greatest players ever to play the game.

LeBron James scored 48 points during Game 5 of the 2007 NBA Eastern Conference Finals.

Let's Get Active!

People like basketball because it does not require lots of gear. All you need is a ball and a court. You can play informal games, such as a one-on-one game. One-on-one basketball is a special game played by two players. It is a great way to practice shooting, dribbling, and stealing.

You can also join, or become a member of, a basketball team. You can do a search on the Internet to find out how to join a team in your area or at your school. Basketball is a lot of fun to play, whether on a team or shooting baskets with your friends!

Glossary

bounce (BOWNS) To spring up, down, or to the side.

cheating (CHEET-ing) Acting dishonestly.

college (KAH-lij) A school one can go to after high school.

contests (KAHN-tests) Games in which two or more people try to win.

defense (DEE-fents) When a team tries to stop the other team from scoring.

foul (FOWL) Breaking the rules of a sport or game.

informal (in-FOR-mul) Not following a special set of rules.

offensive (AH-fent-siv) When a team tries to score points in a game.

official (uh-FIH-shul) Someone who has authority.

professional (pruh-FESH-nul) Someone who is paid for what he or she does.

spectator (SPEK-tay-ter) A person who sees or watches something without taking an active part.

strategy (STRA-tuh-jee) Planning and directing different plays in team sports.

whistle (HWIH-sul) A tube that makes sounds when air is blown through it.

Index

Web Sites

Due to the changing nature of Internet links, PowerKids Press has developed an online list of Web sites related to the subject of this book. This site is updated regularly. Please use this link to access the list:

www.powerkidslinks.com/lga/bask/